Museum of the Soon to Depart

Books by Andy Young

All Night It Is Morning
Museum of the Soon to Depart

Chapbooks

mine
All Fires the Fire
The People Is Singular
John Swenson Dynamicron

Museum of the Soon to Depart

Andy Young

Carnegie Mellon University Press
Pittsburgh 2024

Acknowledgments

Gratitude to the editors of the following publications for including these poems:

Bellingham Review: "*Fever Within*"; *Consequence Magazine*: "Tableau"; *The Cortland Review*: "night terror"; *Dialogist*: "Phantom Ekphrastic"; *Drunken Boat*: "Display"; *Ecotone*: "Nursling," "Bats after the Hurricane"; *Eunoia Review*: "On Your First Visit since the Revolution. . . ."; *Hymn for the Living Poet: (Verse of April)*: "*Abandoning the Land in Ecuador*"; *Ice Floe Press*: "My Mother's Skull Is Opened the First Time," "Bird Watching," "Grief Walk," "Pandemic Funeral"; *Identity Theory*: "Boraq on Mohamed Mahmoud Street"; *Journal of the American Medical Association*: "Recurrence"; *Michigan Quarterly Review*: "It Is Better to Pray than to Sleep"; *Missouri Review* (Poem of the Week): "Pharmacy Museum Tour Guide, New Orleans"; *The Museum of Americana*: "Old City Cemetery" (parts 1 and 2); *One*: "Pest House Sketches: *The Pest House at Jaffa*" (part 2 of poem); *Pank*: "Grief during Carnival Season," "Picasso's Kitchen"; *Peauxdunque Review*: "Raw Wool at Kustanai Textile Processing Plant," "*Shattered*," "Villanelle of Her Absence," "Botero's *El Gato del Raval*"; *Prairie Schooner*: "St. Joseph's, Star of the Sea"; *Radar*: "Museum of Mourning" (part 3 of "Old City Cemetery"); *Southern Humanities Review*: "The Immunity of Dreams"; *storySouth*: "Far from Her in Egypt under Curfew," "Second Clinical Trial"; *Swwim*: "Family Portrait at Golden Mummies of Bahareya"; *Under a Warm Green Linden*: "pinworms," "Bomb Shelter, Plaça del Diamant, Barcelona," "To Your Most Excellent Health"; *The Volta*: "Song of the Plastic Bags"; *Vox Populi*: "Pest House Sketches: *The Pest House at Jaffa*" (part 1 of poem); *Warscapes*: "*Night Walk*," "Cairo as the Counterrevolution Begins"

"My Mother's Skull Is Opened the First Time" and "Villanelle of Her Absence" were runners-up for the 2020 and 2021 Words and Music Writing Competition, respectively. "On Syrian Political Cartoonist. . . ." and "Far from Her in Egypt under Curfew" won the 2015 Nazim Hikmet Poetry Contest. "The Immunity of Dreams" was featured on *Poetry Daily* and was a finalist for *Southern Humanities Review*'s 2017 Auburn Witness Poetry Prize. "Grief during Carnival Season" was a finalist for *Split Lip Magazine*'s 2019 contest. "Tableau" was a finalist for *Consequence Magazine*'s 2017 Women Writing War contest.

Some of these poems were written and/or revised at residencies at Jiwar (Barcelona), the Virginia Center for Creative Arts, and the Kallenberg Artist Tower (Shreveport, Louisiana). I am grateful to the hosts.

Thank you to Peter Cooley, Carolyn Hembree, Brad Richard, Laura Mullen, Kay Murphy, Toi Derricotte, Rodney Jones, Katy Balma, and Allison Campbell for their guidance with these poems and for their solidarity in persevering as poets in these tough years. To Maria Rowan, Eddie Grant, and Joseph Smith for their friendship and belief in my work. To Naomi Shihab Nye for publishing my first poem and for lighting the way. And to Khaled Hegazzi for absolutely everything.

Cover art: © 2024 Josephine Sacabo
Book design: Ellis Jones

Library of Congress Control Number 2024939367
ISBN 978-0-88748-706-4

10 9 8 7 6 5 4 3 2 1

Contents

DISPLAY OF GRIEF

9   Grief during Carnival Season
10   *Abandoning the Land in Ecuador*
12   My Mother's Skull Is Opened the First Time
13   *Shattered*
15   Bomb Shelter, Plaça del Diamant, Barcelona
17   Recurrence
18   Phantom Ekphrastic
19   The Immunity of Dreams
20   Second Clinical Trial
22   Tableau
24   To Your Most Excellent Health
26   Bird Watching
27   Pandemic Funeral
28   Villanelle of Her Absence
29   Grief Walk

HALL OF PESTILENCE AND UNHEALED WOUNDS

33   pinworms
34   *Fever Within*
35   night terror
36   *Raw Wool at Kustanai Textile Processing Plant*
38   Song of the Plastic Bags
39   Bats after the Hurricane
40   Pest House Sketches: *The Pest House at Jaffa*
44   Pharmacy Museum Tour Guide, New Orleans
47   *Night Walk*
48   Boraq on Mohamed Mahmoud Street
50   Cairo as the Counterrevolution Begins
51   Far from Her in Egypt under Curfew
52   Bone Saw Villanelle
53   On Your First Visit since the Revolution,
       We Drink for Four Hours on St. Claude Avenue
54   On Syrian Political Cartoonist Ali Farzat's Self-Portrait,
       Drawn after His Hands Were Broken

ARCHIVES OF PRAYER

59   Family Portrait as the Golden Mummies of Bahareya
61   Display
62   It Is Better to Pray than to Sleep
69   Nursling
70   Picasso's Kitchen
71   Botero's *El Gato del Raval*
73   Ash Wednesday, 2020
74   Old City Cemetery
79   St. Joseph's Day, Star of the Sea

Display of Grief

Grief during Carnival Season

Ninth Ward, New Orleans

My new talent is to stare at exactly nothing,
air like the lead blanket used for X-rays,
blankness passing by my window like a train.

There once was a boy who stopped talking.
Later he said he was in a glass box under the sea
and feared moving would break the glass.

I am that boy. I used to think I would die
of sadness but have learned there is no such luck.
So I sit by the wormy gardenia bush
as bass drum and tuba
thump through the streets—music gone
as soon as it's heard, a gathering mist
on the unvisited graves at St. Roch—
but grief is a labor-like squeezing.

The dead are not picky;
you don't have to wash their grapes.
Across the river, bereft, they blink dumb
in the bright nowhere, stare back at us

where scraps of gold mote the air
over feathered heads and bright trinkets
wink against the sun, a revelry that will end
in ashes thrown into the Mississippi,
ashes smeared on the foreheads of the devout.

I could sleep for centuries
when that darkness comes,
and one day, we all will.
Until then I'll steep in night,
though the Dipper is less
a ladle than an axe: just look
next time how it hacks against
the heavens.
                    A shard of trumpet
pierces the dusk, and all
the once-bodied mothers float past,
their hair in the wind like quicksilver.

Abandoning the Land in Ecuador

photograph by Sebastião Salgado
for Roberta Moore & after Marianne Boruch

the women carry these sacks on their backs
their men in cities
                        Quito
                                    Guayaqhil
                                    port cities
                                                flooding to slum

I might have looked at this one with her
        one of those lost days when we filled in years
        and emptied bottles
            the kids thumping through the house

she stalked bargains to get this book
a book she knew I wanted
        take it for a while she said
                now there's no her to return it to

                        look at the black-haired women
            their heads hidden under rounded
                hats like dark wool Q-tips *fabulous*
        she said or did she
            did we look at this together?
            did we talk about those hats?

around each woman's middle a rope's fixed to hold the sack
so their hands are free beside the patient gray donkeys
        all intent to stay on this path
        to Chimbote its market already buzzing off in the distance

she always took me to her farmer's market
        filled our arms with bread and peaches
                her fingers perfumed with basil—

the women cross the cloud-shadows
                    that spill into the mountains' creases
            a shroud is about to drop on the sun

10

                    look at that woman
        in the middle of the line—she has a perfect flourish
        at the sack's top fabric
                    or is that just a shape in the grass?

hey sister:
        will you see her
        when you start your slow descent?

        and tell me: what is it tied at your cinch?
                        a small fruit?
        a child shriveled by distance or my faulty sight?

                    Why does the mountain blur
                    to smoke like the need to live
                        I sometimes lack?

Let that cloud above your head be a figure,
let it stand for something,
        let it be an intervention even—

a rift in the surface
an arm stretched out

        oh Jesus let it at least stay a cloud
        not gone
            to gray wash

                    or a drizzle far from here

        where siblings pick bones
        from their mother's ashes

My Mother's Skull Is Opened the First Time

post-surgery scan
shows inflammation
a gray sea around

a dark emptiness
hole where tumor lodged
size of a child's fist

shoving out frontal
lobe tissue where lives
personality

higher level cog-
nitive functioning
no way to excise

pathology says
tentacles return
no matter standard

of care or candles
lit at St. Jude's shrine
my mother's devout

she touches her beads
still takes the wafer
wears lipstick with her

headband of staples

Shattered

photogravure by Josephine Sacabo

the shattering spreads: shards of a halo
there is no crown round this mother and child

instead two Xs and a child's angled star
piss-hued light
    rectangling up
    the Madonna's face

isn't she pretty there, without her nose,
light like tape across her mouth

darkness veils her,
    its hijab shadow striping up through
his hair where she ran her fingers through—

    hieroglyphics of light
    scar her face

brightness puddles around the baby's eye, pokes
from his mouth like a cigarillo

is it gold or pale yellow
splintering through the glass
    where once a bullet
    where once a rock
    where once a violence
a violin
tried to—did it—pierce through
    to their holy rest?

on the other side the child
side-eyes the opening
small bow-mouth effaced

    maybe the bullet hole is an eye

hash marks below in near darkness where
small nails have tried to scrape the night away
    —the baby—he's searching for ways out

he wants to stick his wet finger into the shattered hole
and let it all fall away
    as we stand there bare of filter of medium

touch there where he's smeared
his fingers on the glass
    or where it's scratched if it's scratched
    and not a flaw in my sight
        either way it's what
        the dead must feel looking in at us
shattered glass slivers
    a shard sticks in the fingertip
        you must tip it toward the light
        to pluck it out

filaments of darkness stream up from the child's head
stubble his face his thoughts seething out
    no he is not thinking he is counting
    the marks our days
        through the shattering
        he sees us

Bomb Shelter, Plaça del Diamant, Barcelona

When they were sleeping I'd stick the funnel in their mouths, first one and then the
other, and pour the acid into them and then pour it into myself. . . .
—Mercè Rodoreda, *The Time of the Doves*

a metal sculpture, a woman made of that metal, trying to move through it,
    trying to free herself from it, three doves anchored beside her, unable to fly

two entrances to the bomb shelter, separated in case the plaza was smashed
two to three bombardments per week the guide tells us
    I scribble his words down, little metal doves

it took three years for Hitler, Mussolini, and Franco to break the Republic
    the guide explains, recasting defeat as defiance

        where was the rest of the world we ask
        it was, they said, an internal matter

today flags for Catalonia's independence flap from balconies
    yellow ribbons to free political prisoners
    we will not win but we will not lose either he says

a folding door opens to the shelter with a timeline in photos
    he points out the Coliseum bomb, a soft spreading plume from high above

        an Italian airman took the photo he says
        I think of the bomber stopping to photograph,
            the decision to document the moment

not seen in the photograph:
observers lifted by the blast and impaled on a fence
    one of them close to giving birth

        first city bombed at night
        first city bombed for two years straight
            how quaint the facts in light of barrel bombs in light of

Natalia, the woman in the sculpture, Rodoreda's character made solid,
    trying to run from herself pouring poison

        into her children while they slept
            to keep them from starving
      if they ate, they ate a porridge of wood shavings

Madrid is run by Spanish colonists, the heirs of Franco the guide tells us
to the European Union it's an internal matter

Catalonia jumps and Spain trembles,
he says *we don't want the pieces of the bread, we want the bread*

in a grainy shot of aftermath: red crosses like targets
on helpless medics' hats, haze of stunned faces

not like now: Damascus, say, flattened in a newsfeed,
children picking grass to eat, haze of pixels blipping past
internal matters

1,400 shelters, now all but three are parking garages
what strange fortune to be here, to climb down into the relic,

wired with bulbs now so we can see
the benches, the bricked, useless Catalonian arches,

the shelter's infirmary equipped then
with a water bucket, needles, ripped up shirts

Nazis tried out new bombers on the Spanish population
internal matters Soviets helped the Republic in exchange
for gold ingots and to get rid of their old fleets

at war's end teenage boys were sent to the front,
"the bottle battalion" the people called them,

the starvation, *worse than the bombs,* ended in 1952
we paid for our own bombings until 1967

If you are resting it's because someone is dying in another city

the present tense grows wings, swooshes past
the flightless doves stay flightless

Recurrence

Because I'm a poet I try to make
music of her diagnosis: scan
the adonic of glioblastoma,
terminal cancer, clinical trials.

No music in this diagnosis: scans
show the tumor bed ringed
with chthonic glioblastoma
cells. Radiation and chemo just

slow what the brain tumor will bring.
The cures break down healthy
cells, too: radiated, poisoned, she
tries to pop back up again

between these cures that break her down.
A new tumor emerges in the parietal,
popping back up again
like a nightmare game of *Whac-A-Mole*.

A new tumor emerges in the parietal
like a ghost of its sibling from the temporal,
like a nightmare game of whack-a-mole.
To hell with games and similes.

Siblings, parents: future ghosts; all's temporal.
There's no meter in that music,
To hell with games and similes.
There is no comfort in cureless verse.

There's no meter in this music,
in the adonic of glioblastoma,
no comfort in this cureless verse
that as a poet I can't help but make.

Phantom Ekphrastic

photograph from Sebastião Salgado's *Migrations*

there is a woman holding a plastic leg
            there is your mother soft and draped

        two white sneakers
                        in her other hand

her face turned her head veiled
        her expression pleased it seems

                    she is humming to you
                    telling you everyone who's

waiting to see you at home
        what you will all eat

she stands at your bedside
as she clips your leg back on

            look how she cradles the heel
            like another child

The Immunity of Dreams

I made a house of water for my hands
        my son says, half-submerged
that night his shout wakes me

        from dreams of the salt flats of Siwa
            air like white smoke
                in the distance

                        figures in bright cloth
                        leaning into the wind
                            which takes their voices

how did people know to call it wind
        to call it a thing
            when it was just air moving

        I can't answer

the drowned
                        child face down
                        in the news photo
                            looks like him at two

            I want to eat fire and have it not be hot

a boy five days old
        crossed the sea
            in a life vest

morning questions

        sound of spider steps on metal

            I need some words for Thursday
            I need a string of words to climb

why do you hand me
        this vest a woman asked
            before she saw the child inside it

Second Clinical Trial

My brother sends a picture: our mother
holding a tube up through her soft white hat,
smiling. I think she has her lipstick on.
She's just had a hole bored into her skull.
How lucky I am, she says, *to be in the best hospital,*
the best brain tumor center in the world,
to have the best doctor. They say he worked
on one of the Kennedy's brains.

Fourteen-month median lifespan
and no cure. There's nothing for you
if you don't have a tether to hope.
And so the catheter of polio,
the virus recombined, injected
into the tumor. The body attacks
the virus and kills the tumor.
"It's like polio was made
for this purpose," Dr. Friedman says.

Next shot she's walking out the sliding
doors: vibrant, waving.

But healing brings swelling.
Two weeks later she'll black her eye falling,
barely able to shuffle, slurring
from swelling in the parietal lobe.

I will Google brain maps, read her MRI.
Something presses against the supramarginal
something or other that tells you where
you are in space and against the spot
that registers empathy. Wait. There's
a physical location for empathy?
It can be damaged? I don't know shit.
I don't know how she has her faith, don't
know who she'd be without empathy.

She said when they removed the tube
it felt like a wet piece of spaghetti
coming out of her head.
She says that she's lucky.
It's been a good experience.

Tableau

photograph of Shaimaa El Sabbagh, killed by police in Cairo,
January 24, 2015, *New York Times*

a man holds a woman
around her waist
his eyebrows raised

as in a please a no
this is not the woman's
husband though

that makes the image easier
easier than him home
with their son reading

this man keeps her
from falling her hand
curling as if she's listening

to a pure note of music
feeling for the high screech
of strings or saying

wait wait no
I have a child wait no
I am holding only

a wreath of flowers
for the dead of Tahrir
the curling hand

still grasps the small flag
that says whatever
it says

*   **   *

behind them one in uniform
stands with his clear face
shield lifted to better see

in another shot
a man from the march
stares mid drag

on his cigarette
as if watching
traffic pass

from a stoop
crop out what
happens later

the man lifting her
over his shoulder
carrying her

to the Borsa coffeeshop
crop her death
the ambulance refusing

to help crop the round up
of witnesses zoom in to
the moment Islam Osama

turned his camera just after
the shots it is so
like love their embrace

Hollywood could make
a movie of it is it wrong
to say that it is beautiful

To Your Most Excellent Health

to be alone there
    in the antiseptic
    in the sound of breath machines
            to fight to turn your
        eyes to the voice you
        hear to summon strength
to whisper back *no*

one doctor's giving up
        one doctor offers hope
           like an amulet
           in a small, sealed jar
           we take turns keeping
              in our pocket

alone there
        in the beeps and groans

you see your own mother there
        in the antiseptic
           haughty, mid-stride
           ice cream cone in her hand
             cat-eye glasses a bag at the crook
           of her arm
                behind her an awning
              a shop with shade inside
              cool dark shade to be there to be
      anywhere home has been
      mountains rocky coast close
      quarters at the back of town

to not be alone there
        sound of breath machines
but with your kids
    your brothers

        to not be alone
           in the beeps and groans
           no ungloved touch
           no voice you'd know
           in your deepest sleep

in the video chat
    sound of breath machines
your eyes still dark and huge still sharp
your hair growing back thick and brown
no gray at all you are tough as the skull
against which your brain presses
    lit up white on the scans

alone there
    beeps and groans
  not knowing why no one visits
    though we try to explain

alone in that brightness
    in that antiseptic
  nurses floating around like spacemen
      faces lost in their bright shields
        their voices echoes
          in a deep
            well

Bird Watching

The day after my mother died,
I went to find the Indigo Buntings
and I'm sure one lit
in the branches ahead
but I suck at binoculars.
Over here my mother said.
She was a crow.
Figure out how to see me.
Then she cawed four times,
her eyes drops of ink,
her feathers black and flat
like what? Knives? A night lake?
Who gives a shit.
I don't want poetry now.
I'd selected the oak casket,
helped pick her coffin clothes
through Facetime. Did she
need shoes? A bra? Why
the hell would the dead need bras,
I thought but said *bring it in case.*
I attended the virtual burial,
if one can say it is "attending"
to sit and weep before a screen
where in another, unopened tab
a man on an American street
holds a sign that says
Sacrifice the Weak

Pandemic Funeral

a broken duplex

The day my mother's buried,
light throws itself against the earth.

Light throws itself against the earth,
a bird against a window.

Like birds in a window,
my family's in the screen.

My family inside a screen
for her Facebook funeral.

In a Facebook funeral,
siblings sit a pew apart.

All my siblings pulled apart.
My father's masked and small.

My father, masked: a small
animal from this distance.

A distant animal,
I watch the digital spectacle.

A strange spectacle: a digital burial—
Oh and there're the gravediggers.

Quit that, shovel men, quit
that wet plot where cannot be

that she's not here, that I'm not there.
My mother. What is this plot? It cannot be.

Villanelle of Her Absence

I keep on forgetting my mother is dead.
The fact is sealed: a shard in a vitrine.
Loss sews me up with its surgical threads.

I almost send her a pic of the kids
hugging the dog in the sun. Their sweet grins.
I keep on forgetting my mother is dead.

I send it to my sister. Try to get out of bed.
Light a candle in front of her picture again.
I'm lost; breaking at the sutured threads.

Which saint for students? Which for staying fed?
She knew the saints: more like friends than religion.
I keep on forgetting my mother is dead

until birthdays, Thanksgiving—I'll dread
every time she can no longer be in—
her loss the last gossamer thread

of the time on earth she had to spend
with us. Why didn't I pay attention?
I'll keep on, forgetting my mother is dead.
Loss is remaking me: cloth, filling, thread.

Grief Walk

City Park, New Orleans, Spring 2020

I wanted the night heron to mean something.
I passed it each morning, and it stared
at me with its jeweled eye as if it knew.

I wanted it to be a spirit to guide or comfort.
To warn, even. Turns out it hangs around the bridge
because of the cottonmouth nursery

woven into the bayou's fallen bamboo.
It's there to stalk the hatchlings.
What did I seek wandering the wilds of a city

where cattle egrets huddle in neglected weeds,
beside the I-10 where the city's people
were once left to thirst as they watched

floodwaters swallow their shotgun houses?
As I walk I remember myself,
someone's daughter in the world,

rambling off in a faraway town, the language
I skirted rich and impenetrable as the shadows.
What has happened happened.

Now gorgeous, invasive flowers keel over
above my head, the air roiling
with cobalt dragonflies.

Hall of Pestilence
and Unhealed Wounds

pinworms

come out of the living at night
to lay eggs

        we search our son
for pearlescent threads

in the phone light
    faint smears of shit

in skin slits red crowning
        the cave's entrance

    to rivers of vessel and tissue
rope & sac shaped in my own flesh

    no you bastards you cannot
have him yet

you will have your chance
        with us all one day

his sister stirs
    as we're peering in

will she remember it
        as a piece of dream

    this quiet violation
our search of the boy

who once fed on me for the world
        in him now feeding

Fever Within

Rusted Sheet Metal with Nails, Ronald Lockett

Curled in the center
               she is fixed
         to her
            atmosphere
                  torn strips of silver

peek out to some clear
               place beyond
        where once the silver
            was a tin barn
                holding the hot

hay mouths of young horses
               curved warmth
       of new eggs
            here in the museum
                its edges threaten

to flake to dust
               her spine
        a series of holes
            her outline pocked
                with emptiness

—needles pulled out
               what is not her
        pulls away
            the world curling off
                with its bright rust

leaving her peeled back
               to the substratum
        of fever the clinic
            oxidizing around her
                only her body

pinned down and the tube
               through which a liquid does not
        drip but erodes
            between the silver intervals
                of what nails her there

night terror

open-eyed though open-eyed
     I cannot see it

    another tongue

        back together
  with tape what tape

     a wailing a wailing

   I grew them, breath braiding
   limbs thickening
         and must have

grown this too

or maybe I am just
   a tunnel back
      into the communal horror

Raw Wool at Kustanai Textile Processing Plant

photograph by Sebastião Salgado

the woman wades through what—

    sea fog?
        thick blood?

    she seems to be holding
           a child
                at the breast

    but no
        it's wool she walks through,
                and that's wool
                spilling
                      from her thick arms

she shifts through tumbles of it
using the force of her whole leg
        to slide against the ground—
                something on rails

inside the wool surrounding her:
faces
        reduced to soft blurs
                faces of bodies falling

of sudden violence
of ones who died
        in the middle of living
                with no signs except

intricate symmetries surrounding us

the faces are starting
        to cover her—not faces
        no that's raw wool
        in her hands
            don't make it what it isn't

the *wool* is pulling at her
    or she is pulling
        it toward her,
           a child
           adrift in the river

              or is she the one
              that is drifting?

   she wears a dress with small white dots
       as if she meant to be home laughing

       with her sister
       the kids off somewhere
       tumbling through
           acres of light

there's a round tentacled thing behind her
      we see it but she can't—
          hard plastic shiny
             thing—it dangles its stiff tentacle!

but all she sees is the wool
    she cannot stop
        looking down at

to her, it is water
               she's on a ship
                         ready to leap

Song of the Plastic Bags

on the road to Saqqara
a road beside the road
    or a piled path of rocks
    or oh my trash
        solid seeming

and solid in fact
solid bottles muck cups buckets
    rafted together yes solid
    but step on it and sink
        green between the swill

and hydrocarbons
this is water a finger
    of the Nile snaking along
    beside the road to Memphis's
        necropolis, the oldest pyramid

with its stacked mastabas
its refusal to disappear
    below it the Serapeum vaults
    tombs for the Apis bulls
        actual bulls their tombs

like rooms you could walk in
you can count the stars carved
    into the ceiling
    of the road
        for the dead

and the dead never leave
look the trash is singing for them
    wind's throat through sacs
    polymer polymer polymer
        polypropylene polyethylene

        snagged all down   the barbed wire

Bats after the Hurricane

You'd think us shadows
but our bodies hang,
soft palmfuls of air
emanating heat,
which pours over you,
as from hidden suns,
our five-toed feet curved
round restored, exposed
beams, wings jacketing
bodies, heads pointed
down, numberless
guano colonies
forming beneath us.
The city, upside
down through the windows,
is shedding itself,
buildings stripped bare of
their human makers;
soon we will fill them.

Pest House Sketches: *The Pest House at Jaffa*

First sketch of *Bonaparte Visiting the Victims of the Plague of Jaffa*,
Antoine-Jean Gros, New Orleans Museum of Art's "Orientalism" exhibit

1. First Sketch of the First Sketch

This Napoleon turns his face away
from the slumped
    body he half-holds.

The central figures: Syrians
or so it seems
    from their lack of uniform.

The one in red fixes startled eyes
on the leader
    as if to give a message.

In the Louvre's final, sprawling version
those figures are gone.
    Instead a slumped body tries

to stand as Napoleon reaches out
to touch its wounds.
    That version has an outside

clanging in daylight
beyond the striped arches
    of the mosque turned

military hospital. We'd call
what's outside Tel Aviv now.
    What would we call

the Syrians—Palestinians?
Where do their
    descendants live?

In Damascus maybe
or in a refugee camp
    in Yarmouk

its misery thick and similar
to the plague house,
    a kindred, jaundiced light—

but they are in a future
outside the frame,
    as were the bayonetted

prisoners and the two days
of rape
    and slaughter

Napoleon gave as a gift
to his men. All eyes now
    on the Emperor

in his shaft of light. You
either do or do not think
    he has a right to be there.

2. Second Sketch of the First Sketch

Before the Emperor's commission
was presented at the Paris Salon,
        before the Louvre,
        more plague victims
            clot the edges

of the sketch, and there's no glimpse
of an outside as in the painting:
        a distant burning,
        a French flag
            against the dust.

The country of the sick
is a small one and borders
        nothing. In sallow air,
        the dying blur
            into their own

green shadows. A figure falls
into a sea of half-robed bodies,
        arms fixed in a cross-less
        crucifixion.
            Beige and brown

smudges reach up to the soldiers
as if to beg.
        Whoever they are
        will not make it
            to the final version,

will be painted over
with the bodies the artist
        chooses to save:
        two colorful locals
            who proffer bread,

the afflicted soldiers,
whose buboes
   the leader—
   oh so mercifully—
      reaches out to touch.

Pharmacy Museum Tour Guide, New Orleans

In the glass cases
you'll see the scarrifier, the phleem, the jar of leeches.

Note the self-trepanation gadgets,
 the lead needles with bent tips,
 pigrib toothbrushes invented by a prisoner.

Those globes of liquid in the window front
were dyed to warn:
 red for epidemic,
 yellow for yellow fever.

Imagine the smells with no sewer system,
 wigs held on with lard. Tar-covered bonfires
and cannon shots for the miasma,
 the spirits afflicting the city.

  Those red and white stripes
   on barber poles?
  Bloody rags. Barbers were the ones
   to lance and amputate.

  Eighth-century Baghdad had pharmacies,
 and native people here had herbal cures and ceremonies,
  but the first licensed pharmacy in the U.S. was this one,
  opened in 1816 by Dr. Louis Joseph Dufilho.

Customers sat down at that soda fountain
and had cocaine in their soda—coke—
or maybe a 7-Up:
  Lithium Takes the Ouch Out of Grouch!

  Mercury? For the raging syphilis:
  a night with Venus a lifetime with Mercury—

Don't miss the tonsil guillotine
 —with its little tonsil bucket!
 which made it nice and quick.

Over here the opium tampons
(ladies always let out a sigh when I get to those),
    Belladonna Plaster, Godrey's Cordial,
        laudanum and treacle for the baby.

Just like now people came from far and wide,
some visiting, some in town,
you know, on business—
        around the corner, where the Omni Hotel is now,
        "slaves" were "bought" at the biggest auction in the South. . . .

Of course you want to see more!
    Here's the Blister Beatle, Cantharis—
        what you might know as Spanish Fly.

        The compounding station, behind the curtain,
        was hidden to increase the mystery of the good doctor
            who they say even learned a thing or two
            from the vodou priestesses next-door. . . .

Ladies came for potions, too!
    Love Potion Number 9
    Draw Him to Me
    The Essence of Bend Over

And the wealthy had special ways.
They liked their pills coated
    in chocolate or precious metals,
        so they took their strychnine and liver pills
            again and again, the gold ball tracing
            each intestinal canyon. . . .

    And white ladies liked being a tinge blue—
    a little salve of Nux Vomica on the diaphragm,
        all the rage—
    or they powdered their skin
    with the dust of the Morpho butterfly,
    painted veins on their face
        for that paler, *consumptive* look.

Those stairs over there?
      Might they have led to experiments
      conducted on enslaved bodies?
  Sit down if you feel faint—some say they hear
  muffled screams through the thick wood. . . .
         Oh but that's not the tour
          you signed up for—

Night Walk

painting by Myrtle Von Damitz III

Beneath the cotton-candy pink in the plume
of a tire fire, one man's beard is peeling off.

One looks like a clown, leans on a stick.
Shadow of another the color of fruit rot.

A parade is coming—no it's a crowd
flushed back across the bridge. Pregnant

woman, old man, limping child, a tall one whose
skin's too tight; the bones poke through, obscene.

"Is there a hospital that will protect their names?"

What is the half-dressed woman doing
by the rail—jumping? Retching?

One's nose is gone. Another's lost his whole face.
Where is the body that arm belongs to?

"Does someone have water?"
"Does someone have gauze?"

The sky black tatters, the moon an acrid smudge,
smoke clots in red siren lights.

"A vinegar rag for the gas?"

A child holds a miniature horse by a flimsy rope.
It's one of the four. Her horsemen were shot.

There's a clearing over there, but it's above
the river. You'd have to drown to get there.

Boraq on Mohamed Mahmoud Street

graffiti mural by Alaa Awad, Cairo, 2012

      looking back racing forward
   the Boraq can't land her body
a funeral of faces an infant on her
   back whose wings won't work

     her hair splays behind her
such a deep green her legs
her equine body green
   back right hoof that does not kick but flies

    she cannot land lest
she tramples the already
    trampled angled limbs calm
      battered faces floating where
       they reach from concrete
           as from a sea

nearby it's said humans
   sprang from the creator's tears
now dust of factories truck exhaust a market for caged lizards
tomato vendors piles of olives bean hawkers traffic horns
             obliterate the clank of
      swords

here near Metro near KFC the revolution's street battles
     cops and batons against corrugated metal
    from street signs torn down
to shield the unarmed

         her body runs her head
   looks back looks down
where faces haunt red paint two faint
   women shrinking behind the baltagaya
   somebody's man charging sword-first
        head already a skull
         a panther

leaps to reach the women drowning
in black scratches but the Boraq
            looks past them to the limbs of those
                        flying off in winds of blood

Cairo as the Counterrevolution Begins

December 2012

If we'd gone to Alexandria
to breathe the salt air, to be
with our friends as we planned,
we would have checked into that same
hotel off Nebi Daniel. Smelled
the burning cars yards away,
perhaps seen the bearded men
as they stormed the crowd
with machetes. If, as is likely,
I'd have hidden with the kids
and watched from that third floor
window of the room we would
have requested as it faces
the side alley and not the
Mediterranean and the corniche
and its endless car horns, we'd
have seen the knives, the charge
and retreat, the inexplicable ladder-
wielding. I'd have had to try
to come up with an explanation
as to why we were not leaving
the hotel, as to why the shouting,
the smoke, the breaking glass.
Some English-language channel
might have been on television
(is there a television in that room?)
breaking with news from back
in the States. Instead, we stayed
in Cairo, took a drive around to see
the tanks amassing near the poll stations,
picked up some lights to wrap
around the potted fir we found.

Far from Her in Egypt under Curfew

for Iman

We cut lemons in case of gas
before we went to the Square,
wrapped them in our scarves—
the small, thin triangular ones
she said were for people
of the Book. Wearing one,
I could be any one of the three
religions, she said, though
her Egyptian self is seen
as foreign: her clothes,
her ways, her spot-on
English, and I am always
stared at, an *agnabi,* though
I'm told I have *an Egyptian face.*

Those magnetic paper dolls
on my fridge reminded her
of that video, she said,
the headless kid in Syria,
the father holding her
up, looking into where
her face would have been—
is it wrong now to remember
the ishta, its perfumed cream,
its seeds something we could spoon?
Remember the afternoon light flat
and bright as a copper plate, clamor
of men hawking tomatoes, water,
a stone wheel to sharpen knives,
the voice of that man shuffling,
his hands out, his cry
catching in his throat
Ya Raab Ya Raab Ya Raab

Bone Saw Villanelle

My friend, an AIDS survivor, will be cut to the bone
again today. He'll be short another digit.
Surely by now you're a pro at amputation.

Khashoggi's fingers were sawed off one by one.
As the forensic doctor worked, he listened to music
—one needs focus while cutting to the bone.

Who will take the blame? Not son
of a king not king—oil and cash make all legit
as democracy's drugs kick in for amputation.

*A hell of a lot better than the whole
foot,* says my friend. *It's not like I can quit
because they cut me to the bone.*

In the museum, the Victorian cutting saw shone
with its curved jade handle. He asked me to snap a pic,
stunned by beauty paired with amputation.

We wait for updates on Twitter, by phone.
Half of us half-here, half not giving a shit
because either way they'll cut us to the bone;
each day is its own amputation.

On Your First Visit since the Revolution, We Drink for Four Hours on St. Claude Avenue

for Ehab

You hate that I teach
the Romantics, even
the disillusioned ones
so riddled with hope—
you use your mind to form

a shield, you say. That's how
you weren't shot like the seven
you stood next to in the Square,
how you fend off the fangs
of *was it worth it.* Back in Cairo,

your friend asks you to take him
to his shock treatments, the only thing
he says can shake him free
of a weight that crushed him '
even before Shaimaa was shot.

The bottle gets emptier. We taste
the whole grape in our mouths.
For a moment you are not hopeless,
more like *a man / Flying from something
that he dreads,* and we talk of how

you'll change your life, you'll cook
and draw again, drink less, smoke less,
try not to wish things worse so that people
will rise up again—two bottles in
and words swirl *shock   shield*

crush   dread   thawra
I search your mouth
our words for something
to clutch: *Riddled.*
There's a word, I say.
Yes, you say, there's a word.

On Syrian Political Cartoonist Ali Farzat's Self-Portrait, Drawn after His Hands Were Broken

his lips drag down his gaze
straight revealing the sneer
that might otherwise be taken
    as the sadness of Damascus
    where he was left
        in a heap on the street

praise the sneer the wilting gaze
he ringed his left eye
with ink to show the bruising
    creased his face and pillow
    with lines jagged as stones
        filled in the dip of his

own neck the tube in the crook
of his arm praise the exactitude
his hands mummy-wrapped
    broken fingers halved
    by tape and gauze somehow
        he unbent the middle finger

of the right hand made it jut
praise the unbending above
the others away from his body
    in two dimensions it points
    to the heart praise the heart
        maybe the finger really

didn't unbend maybe it's one
of the fingers which does not
work now this is a self-portrait
    how he sees himself
    how he wants to be seen
        in any case he perched

a pen praise the pen managed
to shade his hair black and gray
his burned beard his posture
    wincing against sheets praise
    the sheets on which he rests
        the sheets on which

he draws himself praise
the ink the printing presses
churning in hidden rooms
 the smudges on hands
 after touching news
  praise food stalls

in occupied squares praise
concrete pilings that smash
down walls praise bandanas
 soaked in vinegar
 praise Fridays
  of chanting

and chanting again knowing
nothing will change anytime
soon praise the cartoons
 of Ali Farzat
 praise Ali Farzat's
  middle finger

Archives of Prayer

Family Portrait as the Golden Mummies of Bahareya

A couple faces one another
as if in conversation.
This is how they were found.

Now they lie in vitrines
like fish in facing tanks.
Could not speak if they

could speak. They were
dressed for their death passage,
not to be specimens in glass.

Her bare breasts shine
like doorknobs. Linen
wraps for the poor, gold

masks for the rich, eyes
so lifelike excavators
gasped when they brushed

the dust away. The revolution
left no money for excavation;
thousands of mummies

still lie in burrowed tunnels
under the houses and roads.
The dead do not ponder

revolutions, but they like
to sometimes be considered.
Small mourning statues

were found in the tombs,
meant to eternally weep
at their side. One man

is a merchant with a Horus crown.
Ptolemaic, someone says.
Our son points to another's

thickly outlined eyes.
He is awake he says
but does not answer.

A stone girl, five years old,
too poor for a golden crown:
my daughter, also five,

asks if they're the same
size—yes, almost exactly.
For a while, this is how

our children will think of death:
gilded bodies that keep their shape,
wide-eyed and adored.

Display

Museum of Egyptian Antiquities, Cairo

After they liquefied the brain
and rivered it through the nose,
    after they perfumed and wrapped
the body at the opening-the-mouth
    ceremony, the pharaoh stepped
    into his new bodiless life.

Things of the body remained:
offerings of figs, a golden goose head,
    a stone version of himself
so he could one day re-enter
    and have a face to look out from.
    But a pharaoh who cannot move

cannot touch a horse's mane,
the queen's breast, his ruling scepter.
    He watched the Theban
builders lazing on bricks,
    his second life
    a one-way mirror.

When his mummy was moved
to Cairo, he floated, untethered
    without it, wafting up
the Nile like a hot air balloon.
    Then he found his painted
    eyes staring up at him,

gold body dulled by glass. Rejoined,
he looked up at the faces staring in,
    chewing gum, year after year,
until the millions flooded the streets,
    linking hands around him,
    coughing in tear gas clouds.

It Is Better to Pray than to Sleep

Cairo, 2013

El-Fagr / Dawn

       God creates sun creates moon
              cries the muezzin
         God creates and creates and creates

*

a man hauls a flat cart
filled with broken pots

       broken bike wheels

       broken boots

          bikya bikya bikya

     his voice clatters down the street

       rises up through broken windows

         his wheels write
            lines in the dust

*

someone dreams a truck hitting a building
    one a quick earthquake
another: people stomping
       all at once on the floor above

the bomb less a sound from a distance
    than a feeling of being shaken
by the shoulders quick and hard
       by invisible hands

most sleep through
    like the dead
get up dressed
      go to work etc.

"stay vigilant" the embassy
says "stay safe"

    sniff dogs pull at their leashes
        in the station

*

10:30 Nameless Prayer

    for the ones that did not make it
        to the dawn prayer

*

dust storms redden the sky

soon *eid al-adha*
    feast of the sacrifice

soon the slaughter

meat in the hands of the poor

first sun
crowning
    the street in a pool of blood

*

El Zoohr / Noon

    in the black fields
    the farmer's day
    is done

*

the Friday call
    floods the street
    with the faithful

      streaming toward the mosque
      but not
          a boy

hands in dirt
    his head bent
          over
      his father's shovel

      vegetable vendor
          exclamatory purple of eggplants
              small hard limes dot dot dot
                ... ellipses ...

          (parenthesis
              of bananas)

                    (huddled whispers)

*

El-'Asr / Afternoon

at the protest locked gates around the burnt
husks of the old regime

    chants of the crowd a faint roar
    farther out: a roar we can't hear

    one eats a literal heart
    one's about to be burned

the beaten shield of the sun
clatters on the stones

*

64

El Maghreb / Sunset

heat lessens its grip
the sun sheds
       its spent shell

walk out it won't
       kill you
       now

*

dream of the Blue Mosque

gulls swoop over
       the dome
              as if it were a sea

minarets puncture the gray

       a single call to prayer flushes
              out those not there

       to pray
              but to stare
                     into the blue dazzle

*

El-'Isha / Night Prayer

       the sun plunges into black

              time to eat come home
                     come home

*

Deep Night No Prayer

tail lights puncture the dust
ripple red through desert dark

    a shining procession

boys on flatbeds
on bags of cement
    cigarette smoke floating out
    from checkered rags
        two asleep
under a plastic tarp
        and blanket-sail

light of an almost-town
        chews through exhaust

beside the road a man stirs
a great silver pot of fava beans

blue scrawl on a cargo truck

    I am not afraid of death
    I am afraid of the tears of my mother

*

    halos of candlelight
hum of generators
    low flying helicopters

    chanting from
back and front
    windows

down with military down
    with brotherhood
TV flicks on six

split-screens
street battles
    army trucks on fire

at night only death
    calls the faithful out to pray

*

fires in the distance
    winter's coming on

behind Mokattam: pocked hill
    once a mountain

they say St. Simon the Tanner
    lifted to show his faith

now crumbled stone quarry
    where Christian zabaleen

live off picked trash

*

Salaht El Ganaaza / Prayer for the Dead

white flags sail over the throngs
a face on each one

    a still-smiling sheikh
    a screaming teenager
    a battered Christian
        with hair like Jesus

white flags of surrender
white flags their winding sheets
white flags blank pages
    of unwritten decrees

*

El-Fagr / Dawn

> the *bikya* man
>> hauls his cart
>
>> crying out for broken things
>
> a sliver of moon
>> spiked
>> to the top
>>> of the mosque

Nursling

Two parts animal, one ether,
my daughter thickens in my arms,
flesh and testament. Thump to thwack our
two hearts. And I'm all, one, neither
her nor me when I must leave her:
a woman tattered and alarmed,
animal-eyed, torn, tethered
to the daughter who thickens in my arms.

Picasso's Kitchen

Museu Picasso, Barcelona

I will suck the bones of the fish flesh
then cast the bones in clay

I will interrogate the plums
with the sun of this bulb

even a saucepan can shout
everything can shout

I shout a round swirl of paint
to make an apricot right in the center

of your wars your morals
to hell with these confines

the lines defined by your limits even
with bread rations I will still live still life

with green lemons and two fish
still life with radishes with conger eels

with snack with jug with green bottles
red bottles blue broken bottles of wine

there will be no face for the woman
with the lemons in her lap I turn

bird flocks into clots of pink and toss them
from a window *having learned nothing*

but to love things and eat them alive

Botero's *El Gato del Raval*

check me out with my cigarette whiskers
    my too-human
    forehead chin bottom lip
        though top lip's all feline my friend
            and so is my backside

sleek flanks of a cheetah
gut too plump for the kids
    who climb on my back
        to straddle and kick

my fat sausage tail
with the smooth beauty of an amputee
    my ass as sexy as your mama's
            used to be

no need to raise the flash
too much brightness and I'll lose my burnish

why yes that is a little round pearl
at my neck on this delicate leather strip
    you wouldn't dare
        attach a leash to

how I love to sashay through alleys
        to better hear those first spoons
tap the bowls when the sun goes down
            maybe suck on a bone
        tossed out with Ramadan mercy

to slink through Señor Gaudí's houses glittering
with shards of factory trash
    laugh at how his Holy Mother's head is spiked
        to keep the pigeons off

poke around Señor Picasso's city drenched in twilight
        a color I wear well

you can keep your other public sculptures
that copper condom flapping by the beach hotels
that ridiculous cucumber please

I know these streets,
    how afternoon slices the buildings
        into banquets of light

the hallways of succulents
    the sound of soles on stone in the stairwells

cats don't care if it's Sunday or June or twenty-first century

    the city spreads below us like a feast
smell the crusted death trumpets
    those bite-sized
        little silver fish—

tell the stories if you want of shadows falling
    across lit thresholds
        of all the poets without hope

    sunlight will photobomb the dust darling

just stop and fall into the
    uncanny valley of my gaze

    let's find a way to sink
    our teeth into this life

Ash Wednesday, 2020

Sitges, Catalunya

We slept to the clatter of the sea
and rose to search for the weeping
drag queens displaying their mourning
behind the king's erect effigy paraded
to the sea and thrown in: procession
of outlandish widowhood, pañuelos
black wigs face nets a parade
of public weeping that we needed
though we couldn't say why
    we'd spoken of Italy—the virus was
just starting there—as we walked the narrow
sea-wet streets the night before, but mostly
we noticed the cobalt blue stitching everything
together, painted strips at the base of things—
we toasted the blue and the Carnival spectacle
    a few weeks later the borders would close
    again the rich decide who lives

Old City Cemetery

"History park" and wedding venue, Lynchburg, Virginia

1.

No one is buried anymore in Lynchburg's Old City Cemetery
       except for pet ashes in the Scatter Garden
       for those who can pay

and the potter's field that keeps filling
       with photos and plastic hearts.

       But among the gravestones
there's a village
of these small museum-houses
       that talk when you push a button.

The Hearse House houses
what else? An old hearse,
sealed behind glass,
       black and elaborate as a beetle.

White horses if the dead were children.
The voice of the house is twangy, over-friendly.
Some cousin who shows up
       and has to make everyone laugh.

The voice explains the method of procession,
       how prolific death was then,

the hearse alone inside
as if it could be in there making breakfast.

Press the button again:
Check out the Pest House Museum
                    to learn about the great doctor John Jay Terrell

2.

The Pest House changed when Dr. John Jay Terrell
took over in 1862, a Quaker who grew up
on Dreaming Creek. He refused to own slaves
but served in the Civil War.

Terrell operated an integrated quarantine
treating both soldier and slave
when all were leveled flat by cholera,
yellow fever, smallpox . . .

with 75 patients he brought the mortality rate
down from 50 percent to 5

How could 75 patients fit in this room
I wonder but yes that's right this happens now too . . .
there's a checkerboard on the floor's dry, white sand
Terrell spread to absorb the stench.

> *Reading the Bible, I learned it from Moses,*
> a voice says of the sand, but it's a different voice
> for Dr. Terrell, a slightly British accent maybe?
> An earnestness for sure, a voice permanently
> half-strangled by a suppressed weeping
> (did he come from central casting)?—

> *Lime and yellow paint on the outside,*
> *black paint on the inside to save the eyes.*
> *Barrels of limewater and linseed oil*
> *for sores so the clothes wouldn't stick.*

Dr. Terrell scooped cool water with a gourd dipper,
put patients on milk and cabbage soup,
fed them from the goosey neck of the invalid feeder.

The difference between medicine and poison?—
the friendly cousin-voice is back—*the dose.*

Take a look at the asthma chair:
a rocker with arms lifted high
to better fill the lungs.
And don't miss the amputation kit,
not so different from the ones we use today!

3.

The Museum of Mourning

has limited hours mostly
    it's sealed shut in the shade
near the Pest House
       where smallpox victims
       languished on sand floors

near the Station House
       with its steamer trunks
and little plaques of doom:
          "found dead on Rail Road
          3 miles from here Frozen."

On the porch the hot wet
       air licks you like a tongue
and there's a miniature house
       with a copper roof
       for cats though none are around.

Glass display: a "cooling casket"
       like a big picnic basket
to carry the unembalmed dead.
          A sign promises a "Christian
          vault" nearby, a gift shop

with "Died and Gone to Heaven" honey
       from white bee boxes
on the grounds where rare species
       of roses grow in rows
       among the dead.

Open the door to the Mourning Museum!
       Let me in to weep
for everything I've lost and broken,
          for every aunt, every pet,
          for my grandfather killed

by the mines, for my nana's
            lost mind and the cut-down
trees of my childhood,
            for the sideways slits
            of goats' eyes

for clusters of figs
            and their jeweled caves,
for childhood dissipating
            like mist from a lake.
            Let me in

to rend my clothes,
            to murmur like water
at its first source, to touch
            the brooches made of hair,
            the ink of the catalogued dead.

St. Joseph's Day, Star of the Sea

St. Roch, New Orleans

I know right from wrong—
St. Joseph always
      fed my children.

On St. Joseph's Day
everyone is fed
who wants to be:
plates of spaghetti, a fava bean for luck.

I stand before the St. Joseph
shrine at the St. Roch Church
      Star of the Sea
      whose priest came to us
last fall
      at 5 AM
            after I'd spent hours
calling churches
            reaching no one I need
a priest for my uncle for my
mother for my uncle
            she is worried
for his soul *I don't know*
when I ask another sister
      if it still counts
            to be blessed after
the heart has stopped
            the blood, cooled, cooling—

      yes says the deep-voiced
Nigerian priest at St. Roch
      but *I will have to come soon*

on the altar: sesame seeds
sprinkled by Sicilian hands
      around the braided loaves
      lamb-shaped cakes
beans to remember
      the drought St. Joseph stopped
      remember the mob who lynched
the survivors' descendants

not far from here *alien hands* said
the flier who rallied them
        blot upon our vaunted civilization

after Katrina the altars in wide white
emergency tents where people who survived
    fed people who survived

inside the tents the long folding tables
    food stacked sardined pasta
spice on the lips
    plastic plate buckled in abundance
like the *tables of God*
    in the streets of Alexandria
when the voice at sunset calls out
    to break the Ramadan fast

on the altar
lilies oranges almond cookies
bread shaped like turtles
        like purses of St. Joseph
        to remember the poor
like the Shroud of Turin: yes
    a shroud of bread

prayer cards of St. Joseph the Father
    Joseph the Worker
        brown-skinned St. Joseph what
        we would call now
a Middle Eastern man

    white candles for our fathers
for my Middle Eastern husband
    for my uncle who was not a believer
        though we held his hand
and prayed around him hallowed
    be thy name people are bartering children
    for safe passage people
are washing up
    like fish

after a spill
watch the world's back turn
turning them back to where they fled
what have we become what have we yet
to become   I shudder to—   shudder before this bread we cannot eat
before this bread we can   this bread called *aish* in Arabic
the word for life also a word
people chanted in the streets

\

Previous titles in the Carnegie Mellon Poetry Series

2010
The Diminishing House, Nicky Beer
A World Remembered, T. Alan Broughton
Say Sand, Daniel Coudriet
Knock Knock, Heather Hartley
In the Land We Imagined Ourselves, Jonathan Johnson
Selected Early Poems: 1958–1983, Greg Kuzma
The Other Life: Selected Poems, Herbert Scott
Admission, Jerry Williams

2011
Having a Little Talk with Capital P Poetry, Jim Daniels
Oz, Nancy Eimers
Working in Flour, Jeff Friedman
Scorpio Rising: Selected Poems, Richard Katrovas
The Politics, Benjamin Paloff
Copperhead, Rachel Richardson

2012
Now Make an Altar, Amy Beeder
Still Some Cake, James Cummins
Comet Scar, James Harms
Early Creatures, Native Gods, K. A. Hays
That Was Oasis, Michael McFee
Blue Rust, Joseph Millar
Spitshine, Anne Marie Rooney
Civil Twilight, Margot Schilpp

2013
Oregon, Henry Carlile
Selvage, Donna Johnson
At the Autopsy of Vaslav Nijinsky, Bridget Lowe

Silvertone, Dzvinia Orlowsky
Fibonacci Batman: New & Selected Poems (1991–2011), Maureen Seaton
When We Were Cherished, Eve Shelnutt
The Fortunate Era, Arthur Smith
Birds of the Air, David Yezzi

2014
Night Bus to the Afterlife, Peter Cooley
Alexandria, Jasmine Bailey
Dear Gravity, Gregory Djanikian
Pretenders, Jeff Friedman
How I Went Red, Maggie Glover
All That Might Be Done, Samuel Green
Man, Ricardo Pau-Llosa
The Wingless, Cecilia Llompart

2015
The Octopus Game, Nicky Beer
The Voices, Michael Dennis Browne
Domestic Garden, John Hoppenthaler
We Mammals in Hospitable Times, Jynne Dilling Martin
And His Orchestra, Benjamin Paloff
Know Thyself, Joyce Peseroff
cadabra, Dan Rosenberg
The Long Haul, Vern Rutsala
Bartram's Garden, Eleanor Stanford

2016
Something Sinister, Hayan Charara
The Spokes of Venus, Rebecca Morgan Frank
Adult Swim, Heather Hartley
Swastika into Lotus, Richard Katrovas
The Nomenclature of Small Things, Lynn Pedersen
Hundred-Year Wave, Rachel Richardson
Where Are We in This Story, Sarah Rosenblatt

Inside Job, John Skoyles
Suddenly It's Evening: Selected Poems, John Skoyles

2017
Disappeared, Jasmine V. Bailey
Custody of the Eyes, Kimberly Burwick
Dream of the Gone-From City, Barbara Edelman
Sometimes We're All Living in a Foreign Country, Rebecca Morgan Frank
Rowing with Wings, James Harms
Windthrow, K. A. Hays
We Were Once Here, Michael McFee
Kingdom, Joseph Millar
The Histories, Jason Whitmarsh

2018
World Without Finishing, Peter Cooley
May Is an Island, Jonathan Johnson
The End of Spectacle, Virginia Konchan
Big Windows, Lauren Moseley
Bad Harvest, Dzvinia Orlowsky
The Turning, Ricardo Pau-Llosa
Immortal Village, Kathryn Rhett
No Beautiful, Anne Marie Rooney
Last City, Brian Sneeden
Imaginal Marriage, Eleanor Stanford
Black Sea, David Yezzi

2019
The Complaints, W. S. Di Piero
Brightword, Kimberly Burwick
Ordinary Chaos, Kimberly Kruge
Blue Flame, Emily Pettit
Afterswarm, Margot Schilpp

2020
Build Me a Boat: Words for Music 1968–2018, Michael Dennis Browne
Sojourners of the In-Between, Gregory Djanikian
The Marksman, Jeff Friedman
Disturbing the Light, Samuel Green
Any God Will Do, Virginia Konchan
My Second Work, Bridget Lowe
Flourish, Dora Malech
Petition, Joyce Peseroff
Take Nothing, Deborah Pope

2021
The One Certain Thing, Peter Cooley
The Knives We Need, Nava EtShalom
Oh You Robot Saints!, Rebecca Morgan Frank
Dark Harvest: New & Selected Poems, 2001–2020, Joseph Millar
Glorious Veils of Diane, Rainie Oet
Yes and No, John Skoyles

2022
Out Beyond the Land, Kimberly Burwick
All the Hanging Wrenches, Barbara Edelman
Anthropocene Lullaby, K. A. Hays
The Woman with a Cat on Her Shoulder, Richard Katrovas
Bel Canto, Virginia Konchan
There's Something They're Not Telling Us, Kimberly Kruge
A Long Time to Be Gone, Michael McFee
Bassinet, Dan Rosenberg

2023
Night Wing over Metropolitan Area, John Hoppenthaler
Phone Ringing in a Dark House, Rolly Kent
Fleeing Actium, Ricardo Pau-Llosa
Approximate Body, Danielle Pieratti
Wild Liar, Deborah Pope

Joy Ride, Ron Slate
That Other Life, Joyce Sutphen
Sonnets with Two Torches and One Cliff, Robert Thomas

2024
Accounting for the Dark, Peter Cooley
Shine, Joseph Millar
Those Absences Now Closest, Dzvinia Orlowsky
Blue Yodel, Eleanor Stanford
Her Breath on the Window, Karenmaria Subach
Museum of the Soon to Depart, Andy Young